Introduction

This volume, the third of a series, has been compiled to offer the reader inspiring and meaningful verses to help respond to the challenges of everyday life with courage, faith and hope.

The selections were not based on the prominence of poets in the literary field, but rather on the Christian message of truth, peace and the hope of eternal joy, so beautifully expressed by many of the published and heretofore unpublished poets of our day.

We are grateful to the publishers who so kindly gave permission for use of some of the works in this book, as well as to the contributing authors without whom this anthology would not have been made possible.

Salesian Missions wishes to thank those who have given their kind permission to reprint material included in this book. Every effort has been made to give proper acknowledgements. Any omissions or errors are deeply regretted, and the publisher, upon notification, will be pleased to make necessary corrections in subsequent editions.

ACKNOWLEDGEMENTS: "There is One" by Fanny Crosby, © 1977 by Hope Pub. Co., Carol Stream, Il.60187 Used by permission. "Two Roads" reprinted from POEMS TO INSPIRE by Nick Kenny by permission of T.S. Denison & Co., Inc. "Prayers Are the Stairs to God" by Helen Steiner Rice is reprinted by permission of Fleming H. Revell Company, Old Tappan, N.J. 07675. "The Good World" by Edgar A. Guest reprinted from THE COLLECTED VERSES OF EDGAR A GUEST © 1934 by permission of Contemporary Books, Chicago, Illinois.

A Treasury of Poems

from the Salesian Collection

Compiled and Edited by
Sara Tarascio

Illustrated by
Marion L. Quimby
and Paul Scully

Table of Contents

for

A Treasury of Poems

from the Salesian Collection

Morning Prayer

Help me use this day so wisely,
  Lord,
  That there will be no sad regret
When evening comes,
   for hours misspent,
  For work undone;
   and let me not forget
That things which seem
   important now to me
  Might dwindle in the light
   of Thy eternity!
So if I've planned this day all wrong,
  Please rearrange it,
   Lord, and make it right;
Just let me glorify Thy name,
  Put first things first.
   I want Thy smile to-night!

Alice Hansche Mortenson

God of the Earth,
The Sky, The Sea

God of the earth, the sky, the sea,
    Maker of all above, below,
Creation lives and moves in Thee;
    Thy present life through all doth flow.

Thy love is in the sun-shine's glow,
    Thy life is in the quickening air;
When lightnings flash and storm winds blow,
    There is Thy power, Thy law is there.

We feel Thy calm at evening's hour,
    Thy grandeur in the march of night,
And when the morning breaks in power,
    We hear Thy word, "Let there be light."

But higher far, and far more clear,
    Thee in man's spirit we behold,
Thine image and Thyself are there, —
    Th' in-dwelling God, proclaimed of old.

Samuel Longfellow

Take up Your Cross

Take up your cross and follow God
And He will lead the way,
To bring you hope and inner strength
To face each new born day.

Take up your cross and follow God
And cast aside your fear,
For when you need a helping hand
He always will be near.

Take up your cross and cast aside
Your gloom and dark despair,
For He will help to ease the pain
That in your heart you bear.

Take up your cross, be not afraid
However dark your plight,
For God will see you through the storm
And be your guiding light.

Harold F. Mohn

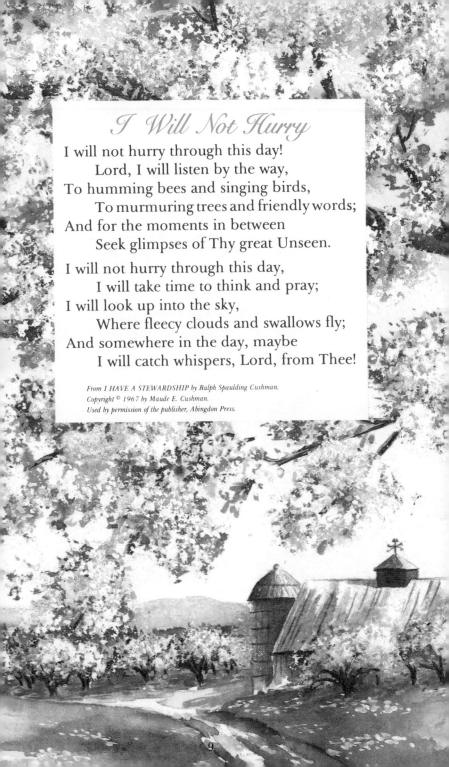

I Will Not Hurry

I will not hurry through this day!
　　Lord, I will listen by the way,
To humming bees and singing birds,
　　To murmuring trees and friendly words;
And for the moments in between
　　Seek glimpses of Thy great Unseen.

I will not hurry through this day,
　　I will take time to think and pray;
I will look up into the sky,
　　Where fleecy clouds and swallows fly;
And somewhere in the day, maybe
　　I will catch whispers, Lord, from Thee!

From I HAVE A STEWARDSHIP by Ralph Spaulding Cushman.
Copyright © 1967 by Maude E. Cushman.
Used by permission of the publisher, Abingdon Press.

A Day at a Time

I don't wish to know tomorrow,
For the trials of today,
Are enough to keep me busy,
Here on life's pathway.

God in all of His wisdom
Could so easily see,
One day at a time,
Was enough for me.

No need to be anxious,
For what the future holds.
God must prepare you,
As each day unfolds.

So Lord, I trust you,
The future is all Thine.
Just help me to live,
One day at a time.

Dottlee Duggan Reid

DISCOVERY

Today I smiled, and all at once
Things didn't look so bad.
Today I shared with someone else,
A bit of hope I had.
Today I sang a little song,
And felt my heart grow light,
And walked a happy little mile,
With not a cloud in sight.

Today I worked with what I had,
Nor longed for any more,
And what had seemed like only weeds,
Were flowers at my door.
Today I loved a little more,
Complained a little less,
And in the giving of myself,
Forgot my weariness.

Grace E. Easley

O Master,
Let Me Walk with Thee

O Master, let me walk with Thee
In lowly paths of service free;
Tell me Thy secret; help me bear
The strain of toil, the fret of care.

Teach me Thy patience; still with Thee
In closer, dearer company,
In work that keeps faith sweet and strong,
In trust that triumphs over wrong.

Washington Gladden

*W*herever He may guide me,
 No want shall turn me back;
My Shepherd is beside me,
 And nothing can I lack.
His wisdom ever waketh,
 His sight is never dim, –
 He knows the way He taketh,
 And I will walk with Him.

A. L. Waring

the Rose

A splendid rose stood
   all alone,
Surrounded by a wall
   of stone.
Around the wall were
   roses, too,
Still neither knew the
   other grew.

So often we, like
   flowers, dwell
Too deep within our
   human shell
And pass through life —
   "not understood" —
Nor making all the friends
   we should.

Anthony J. Pettito

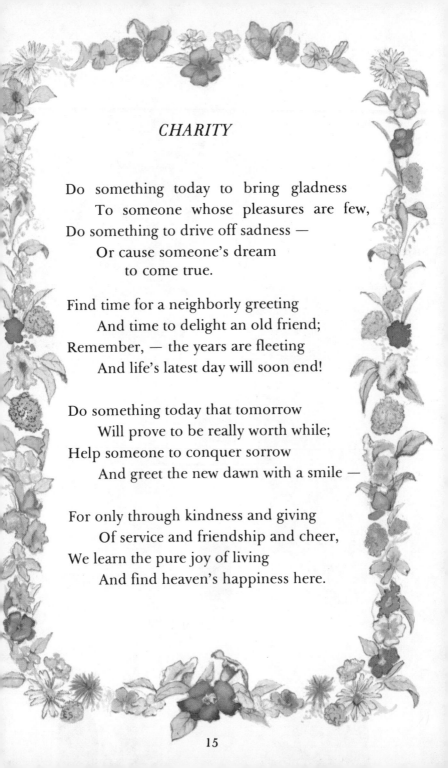

CHARITY

Do something today to bring gladness
    To someone whose pleasures are few,
Do something to drive off sadness —
    Or cause someone's dream
        to come true.

Find time for a neighborly greeting
    And time to delight an old friend;
Remember, — the years are fleeting
    And life's latest day will soon end!

Do something today that tomorrow
    Will prove to be really worth while;
Help someone to conquer sorrow
    And greet the new dawn with a smile —

For only through kindness and giving
    Of service and friendship and cheer,
We learn the pure joy of living
    And find heaven's happiness here.

Listless Moments

Listless moments
spent in flight
Lost forever,
a fool's delight

Lasting moments
Spent in prayer,
Saved forever
in heaven's care.

Bill Twomey

16

COMFORT

Dear Lord, I am so comforted
    in my great love for Thee.
My worries fall like petals
    and my faith burns deep in me.
The thankfulness within my heart,
    the comfort that I feel,
Will lighten every burden
    as in prayer I humbly kneel.
So thankful I am, my dear Lord,
    for each day set apart,
As gratefully my prayers I say,
    with comfort in my heart.
So thankful, I am, my dear Lord,
    I do believe in Thee,
Like Benediction Incense, Thy love
    flows over me.

Charlotte Trevillyan Sheward

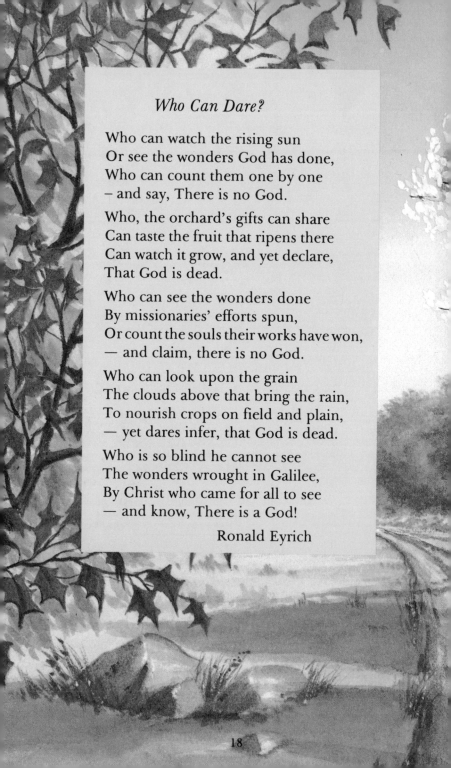

Who Can Dare?

Who can watch the rising sun
Or see the wonders God has done,
Who can count them one by one
– and say, There is no God.

Who, the orchard's gifts can share
Can taste the fruit that ripens there
Can watch it grow, and yet declare,
That God is dead.

Who can see the wonders done
By missionaries' efforts spun,
Or count the souls their works have won,
— and claim, there is no God.

Who can look upon the grain
The clouds above that bring the rain,
To nourish crops on field and plain,
— yet dares infer, that God is dead.

Who is so blind he cannot see
The wonders wrought in Galilee,
By Christ who came for all to see
— and know, There is a God!

Ronald Eyrich

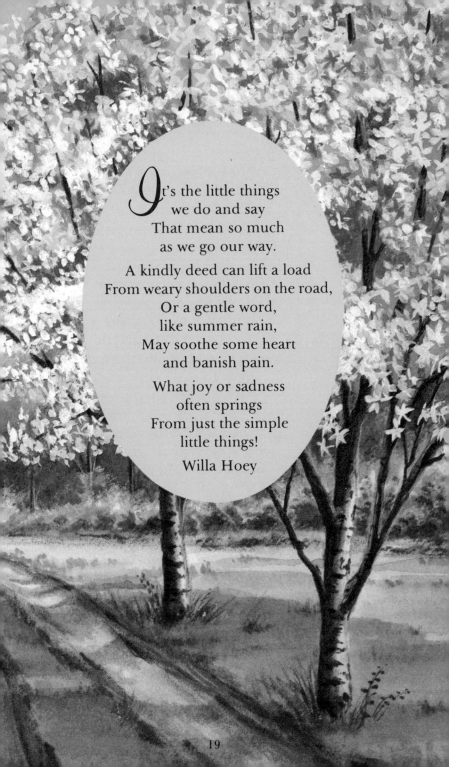

It's the little things
we do and say
That mean so much
as we go our way.

A kindly deed can lift a load
From weary shoulders on the road,
Or a gentle word,
like summer rain,
May soothe some heart
and banish pain.

What joy or sadness
often springs
From just the simple
little things!

Willa Hoey

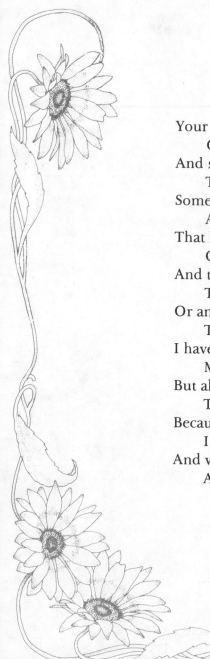

YOUR BLESSING

Your blessing, God, is like a gift
    Of silver and of gold
And sometimes it is almost more
    Than I have strength to hold.
Sometimes You shower so much joy
    And happiness on me
That life is like a paradise
    Of perfect ecstasy.
And that is why I do not mind
    The lightning and the rain
Or any hail or thunderbolt
    That shakes my window-pane.
I have my disappointments and
    My share of earthly grief
But always I remember, God
    That there is some relief.
Because when I have said my prayer
    I hear Your soft reply
And when I lift my eyes I see
    A rainbow in the sky.

James J. Metcalfe

He Is There

He is there, when problems
    surround your life . . .
He is there, when your troubles
    bring worry and strife . . .
He is there, in the darkest
    hour of need . . .
He is there, when all seems lost,
    if only you'll heed . . .
He is there, just listen for
    His word, feel His touch . . .

He is there, just because He
    loves you so much . . .
He is there to calm all the
    fear and the care . . .
He is there, and you can know
    that He'll always be there . . .
He is there, in your heart
    to comfort and uplift . . .
He is there, now and always,
    your greatest gift.

Susan E. Muldoon

There's a Reason

For every pain that we must bear,
For every burden, every care,
    There's a reason.

For every grief that bows the head,
For every teardrop that is shed,
    There's a reason.

For every hurt, for every plight,
For every lonely pain-racked night,
    There's a reason.

But if we trust God as we should,
It all will work out for our good.
    He knows the reason.

*". . . We know that for those who love
God all things work together unto
good . . ."*   *(Romans VIII 28).*

A Song in My Heart

I was thinking of the heartaches
    That I had held so fast
All the disappointments
    That seemed to me so vast.

Nothing seemed to ease the pain
    Of worry held so long
My heart was oh, so weary
    And empty of its song.

I turned my eyes toward Heaven
    And went to Him in prayer
I poured out all my troubles
    And found contentment there.

I forgave all I remembered;
    The things that had been done
I also asked forgiveness
    For remembering every one.

I rose from prayer contented
    I barely remembered the start
Of my troubled soul so weary
    I had a song in my heart.

Virginia Laws

MY SOUL AND I

Know well, my soul, God's hand controls
    Whate'er thou fearest;
Round Him in calmest music rolls
    Whate'er thou hearest.

What to thee is shadow, to Him is day,
    And the end He knoweth,
And not on a blind and aimless way
    The spirit goeth.

Nothing before, nothing behind;
    The steps of Faith
Fall on the seeming void, and find
    The rock beneath.

            John Greenleaf Whittier

The Covert of Thy Wings

I do not even ask, dear Lord,
    That Thou should'st still the sea,
But that Thy strong unfailing love
    With peace abide in me,
For well I know no storm would come
    Could I not stand the test,
So let me lean with faith serene
    Against Thy loving breast;
Willing thus to stand the storm
    Though bruised by grief and pain,
Knowing that someday my loss
    Will prove eternal gain.

For oh, I know no song-filled sky
    Or days all bright and clear
Could ever cause my soul to cling
    To Thee like this — so near.
And had I been less tempest-tossed
    My heart could not have known
The utter sweetness just to trust
    In Thee, and Thee alone!
And so I do not ask to fly
    Above the storm and sing:
Just let me in the tempest feel
    The covert of Thy wings!

        Alice Hansche Mortenson

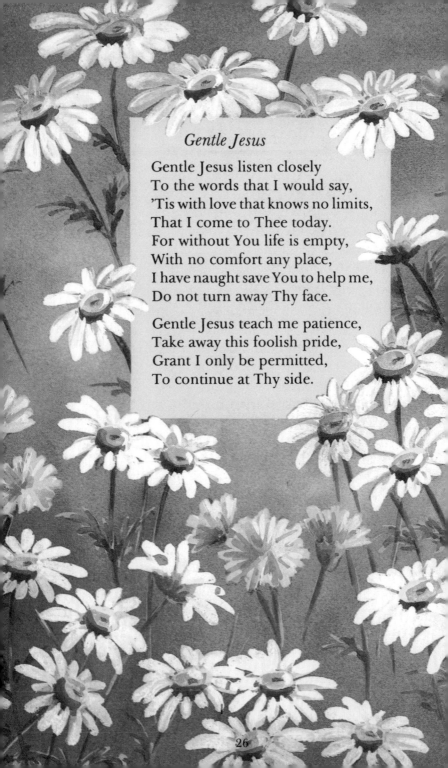

Gentle Jesus

Gentle Jesus listen closely
To the words that I would say,
'Tis with love that knows no limits,
That I come to Thee today.
For without You life is empty,
With no comfort any place,
I have naught save You to help me,
Do not turn away Thy face.

Gentle Jesus teach me patience,
Take away this foolish pride,
Grant I only be permitted,
To continue at Thy side.

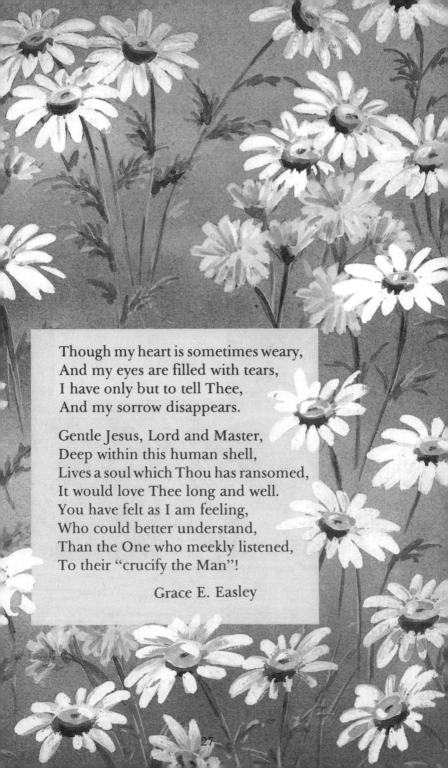

Though my heart is sometimes weary,
And my eyes are filled with tears,
I have only but to tell Thee,
And my sorrow disappears.

Gentle Jesus, Lord and Master,
Deep within this human shell,
Lives a soul which Thou has ransomed,
It would love Thee long and well.
You have felt as I am feeling,
Who could better understand,
Than the One who meekly listened,
To their "crucify the Man"!

Grace E. Easley

All May Be One

Jesus prayed
that all may be one,
like His coat
woven without seam;
but men without love
divided remain,
like His garments
parted at the cross.

Edward A. Gloeggler

If we could see beyond today
    As God can see,
If all the clouds should roll away,
    The shadows flee;
O'er present griefs we would not fret,
Each sorrow we would soon forget,
For many joys are waiting yet
    For you and me.

If we could know beyond today
    As God doth know,
Why dearest treasures pass away,
    And tears must flow;
And why the darkness leads to light,
Why dreary days will soon grow bright,
Some day life's wrong will be made right,
    Faith tells us so.

If we could see, if we could know
    We often say,
But God in love a veil doth throw
    Across our way.
We cannot see what lies before,
And so we cling to Him the more,
He leads us till this life is o'er,
    Trust and obey.

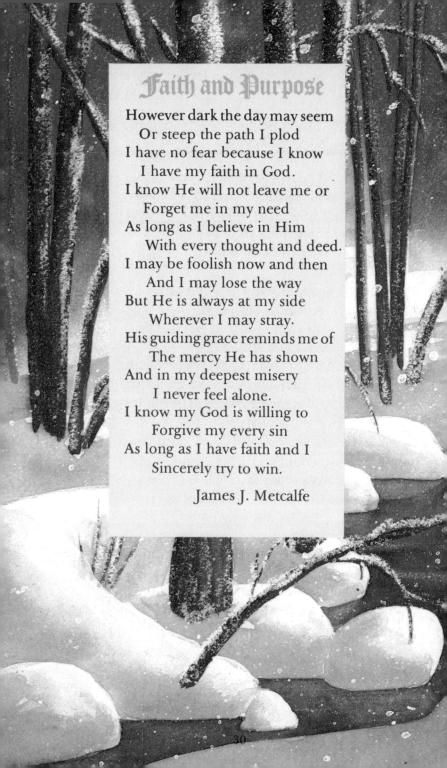

Faith and Purpose

However dark the day may seem
    Or steep the path I plod
I have no fear because I know
    I have my faith in God.
I know He will not leave me or
    Forget me in my need
As long as I believe in Him
    With every thought and deed.
I may be foolish now and then
    And I may lose the way
But He is always at my side
    Wherever I may stray.
His guiding grace reminds me of
    The mercy He has shown
And in my deepest misery
    I never feel alone.
I know my God is willing to
    Forgive my every sin
As long as I have faith and I
    Sincerely try to win.

James J. Metcalfe

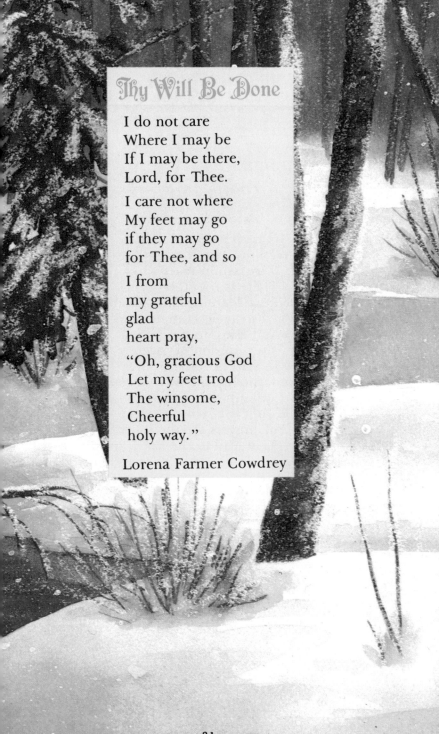

Thy Will Be Done

I do not care
Where I may be
If I may be there,
Lord, for Thee.

I care not where
My feet may go
if they may go
for Thee, and so

I from
my grateful
glad
heart pray,

"Oh, gracious God
Let my feet trod
The winsome,
Cheerful
holy way."

Lorena Farmer Cowdrey

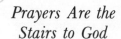

*Prayers Are the
Stairs to God*

Prayers are the stairs
We must climb every day,
If we would reach God
There is no other way,
For we learn to know God
When we meet Him in prayer
And ask him to lighten
Our burden of care –
So start in the morning
And, though the way's steep,
Climb ever upward
'Til your eyes close in sleep –
For prayers are the stairs
That lead to the Lord,
And to meet Him in prayer
Is the climber's reward.

Helen Steiner Rice

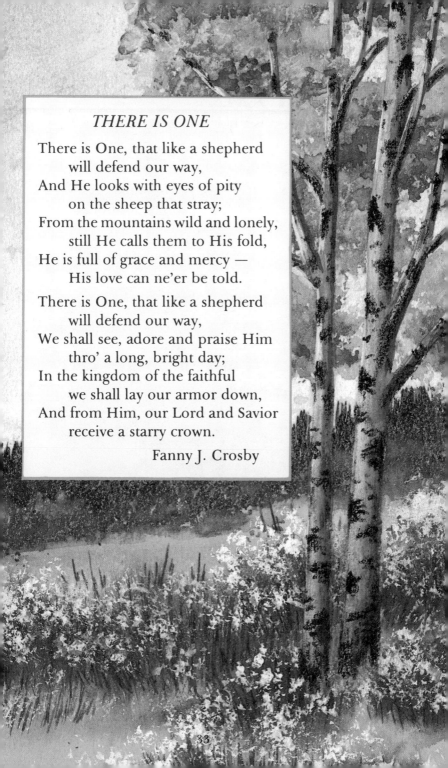

THERE IS ONE

There is One, that like a shepherd
　　will defend our way,
And He looks with eyes of pity
　　on the sheep that stray;
From the mountains wild and lonely,
　　still He calls them to His fold,
He is full of grace and mercy —
　　His love can ne'er be told.

There is One, that like a shepherd
　　will defend our way,
We shall see, adore and praise Him
　　thro' a long, bright day;
In the kingdom of the faithful
　　we shall lay our armor down,
And from Him, our Lord and Savior
　　receive a starry crown.

　　　　　　　Fanny J. Crosby

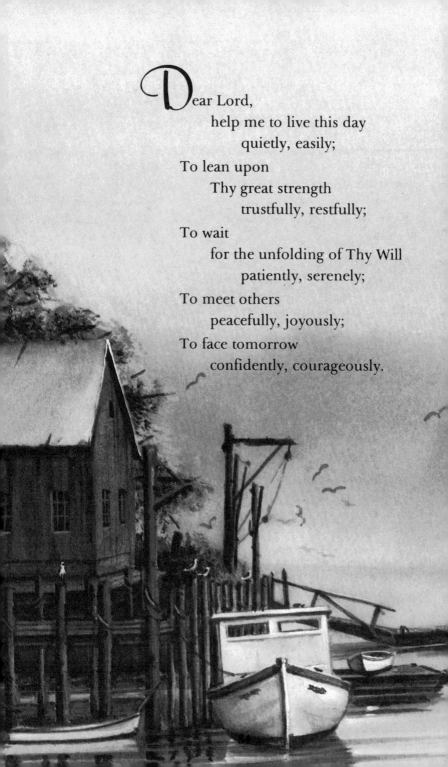

Dear Lord,
    help me to live this day
        quietly, easily;
To lean upon
    Thy great strength
        trustfully, restfully;
To wait
    for the unfolding of Thy Will
        patiently, serenely;
To meet others
    peacefully, joyously;
To face tomorrow
    confidently, courageously.

His Guiding Hand

With outstretched hand, He leads me
Where deep blue waters flow,
When my footsteps tend to falter,
He shows The Way to go.

Gently leading on a journey
Which is yet unknown to me
For the path is steep and narrow
Difficult for me to see.

But I feel my faith grow stronger
And I see a light divine
As I smile and travel onward
With His strong hand holding mine.

Juanita R. Davis

The Zest of Life

Let me but live from year to year,
    With forward face and unreluctant soul.
Not hastening to, nor turning from the goal;
    Not mourning for the things that disappear
In the dim past, nor holding back in fear
    From what the future veils; but with a whole
And happy heart, that pays its toll
    To youth and age, and travels on with cheer.
So let the way wind up the hill or down,
    Through rough or smooth, the journey will be joy;
Still seeking what I sought when but a boy,
    New friendship, high adventure, and a crown,
I shall grow old, but never lose life's zest,
    Because the road's last turn will be the best.

Henry Van Dyke

Give Me a Song

Lord give me a song to lift my soul,
When muscles shrink and dreams grow old,
A melody whose words ring true,
In "this vale of tears" I'm walking through.
Lord give me a song that's made to share
With lonely people everywhere,
Joyous notes on wings that reach
Into the private lives of each.

Lord give me a song that gathers up
Life's sweetest memories in its cup,
Of gentle faces, and a host
Of things now gone but never lost.
Lord give me a song to make my day
A better one in every way,
Fill it with thanks to You who bring
So much of which we ought to sing.

Lord give me a song when skies are grey,
And it looks like winter's here to stay,
When the rain runs down my window pane,
And it seems the sun won't shine again.
How well I can recall the saying,
That "he who sings is doubly praying",
My words might be too low to hear,
But I know a song will reach Your ear.

Lord give me a song that never ends,
And as each silver note ascends,
Perhaps some stranger passing by,
Might gain new courage, such as I.
I do not ask for wealth and such,
For earthly goods don't matter much,
I only pray I may be given
A song, to sing me into Heaven.

                                    Grace E. Easley

Talk it Over With God

You're worried and troubled
    about everything,
Wondering and fearing
    what tomorrow will bring —
You long to tell someone
    for you feel so alone,
But your friends are all burdened
    with cares of their own —
There is only one place
    and only one friend
Who is never too busy
    and you can always depend
That He will be waiting
    with arms open wide
To hear all your troubles
    that you came to confide —
For the heavenly Father
    will always be there
When you seek Him and find Him
    at the Altar of Prayer.

Helen Steiner Rice

God at Our Side

God is forever at our side
    Wherever we may be,
In every happy moment and
    In time of tragedy,

In every disappointment and
    Each wonderful surprise,
And all the lonely moments that
    Are filled with tears and sighs.

In every shadow on the path
    Where we may walk today,
And to the farthest corner of
    The world where we may stray.

God hears our every whisper, and
    He listens to each prayer,
And so we have no reason to
    Be sad or to despair.

God is forever at our side
    We have no need to fear,
As much as we have faith in Him
    And we are real sincere.

                James J. Metcalfe

One Day at a Time

We worry about our tomorrows
Oft missing the joys of today
Troubled about what may happen
Yet tomorrow, may not come our way.

Life's pathway is ever uncertain
"Right now" is what's yours and mine.
The future is safe in God's keeping
We can live but one day at a time.

Gert Holaday

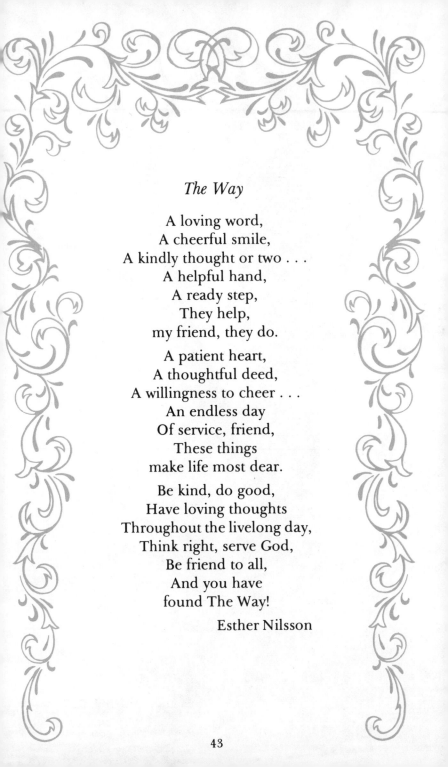

The Way

A loving word,
A cheerful smile,
A kindly thought or two . . .
A helpful hand,
A ready step,
They help,
my friend, they do.

A patient heart,
A thoughtful deed,
A willingness to cheer . . .
An endless day
Of service, friend,
These things
make life most dear.

Be kind, do good,
Have loving thoughts
Throughout the livelong day,
Think right, serve God,
Be friend to all,
And you have
found The Way!

Esther Nilsson

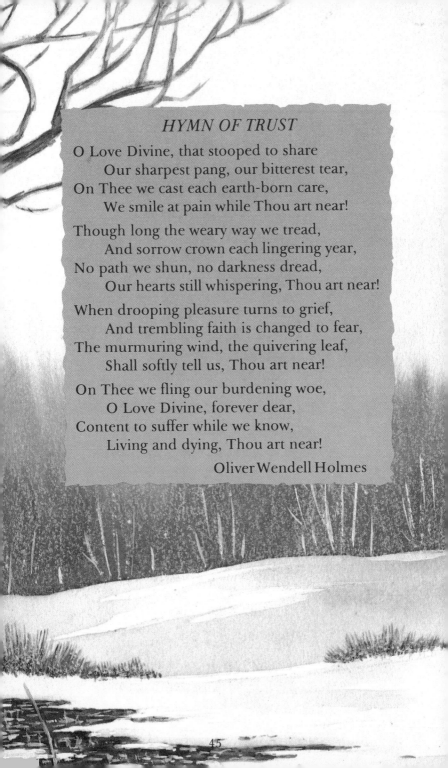

HYMN OF TRUST

O Love Divine, that stooped to share
    Our sharpest pang, our bitterest tear,
On Thee we cast each earth-born care,
    We smile at pain while Thou art near!

Though long the weary way we tread,
    And sorrow crown each lingering year,
No path we shun, no darkness dread,
    Our hearts still whispering, Thou art near!

When drooping pleasure turns to grief,
    And trembling faith is changed to fear,
The murmuring wind, the quivering leaf,
    Shall softly tell us, Thou art near!

On Thee we fling our burdening woe,
    O Love Divine, forever dear,
Content to suffer while we know,
    Living and dying, Thou art near!

                   Oliver Wendell Holmes

COMFORT

When your heart is sad and lonely,
　　And your friends seem far away,
Turn to Him Who is all holy,
　　And He'll drive your cares away.

When a dear one seems to fail you,
　　When for friendship true you long,
Confide in Him Who is all true,
　　And He'll right your every wrong.

Jesus' heart is your true refuge,
　　To Him you can always flee,
Even when your hopes are sinking,
　　He will then a True Friend be.

He will soothe your lonely spirit,
　　He will love and bless and say,
"Come to Me and I will comfort
　　You, today and every day."

If we could just for one moment see
    Into the vastness of eternity,
Most of us would change our ways
    To make the best of all our days.

Each thoughtless word, we so regret,
    Those little hurts we can't forget
Would seem so small in retrospect
    We'd have no time to so reflect.

We'd know the source from which love springs,
    We'd make the most of worthwhile things,
We'd see how best that we could be
    Preparing for eternity.

Clarence Bertram Dennison

A Little Pool of Quietness

A little pool of quietness
    Abides within my heart;
A well of deep serenity,
    Untroubled, set apart
From all the outer world's unrest,
    Anxiety, and care;
And when I turn prayer's golden key
    I find Him waiting there.

A little pool of quietness
    Set deep within the Rock
Of Ages to withstand the stress,
    The pressure, and the shock
Of these dark days in which we live.
    No bomb, no gun can blast
This shelter of His love for me;
    It will forever last.

      Alice Hansche Mortenson

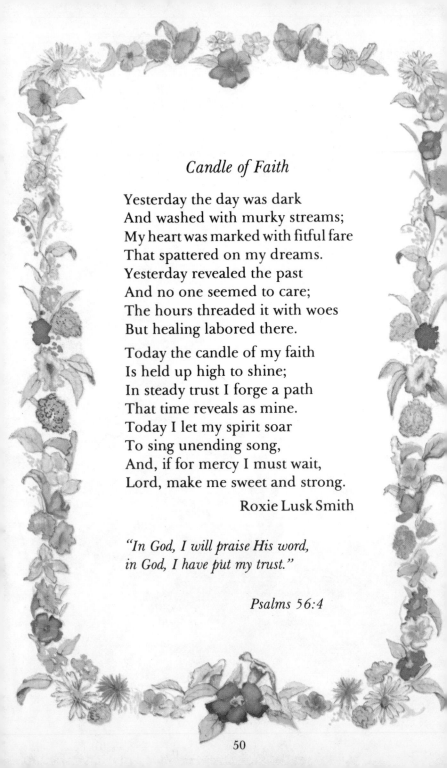

Candle of Faith

Yesterday the day was dark
And washed with murky streams;
My heart was marked with fitful fare
That spattered on my dreams.
Yesterday revealed the past
And no one seemed to care;
The hours threaded it with woes
But healing labored there.

Today the candle of my faith
Is held up high to shine;
In steady trust I forge a path
That time reveals as mine.
Today I let my spirit soar
To sing unending song,
And, if for mercy I must wait,
Lord, make me sweet and strong.

Roxie Lusk Smith

*"In God, I will praise His word,
in God, I have put my trust."*

Psalms 56:4

50

There is One Who Cares

There is One whom we can lean upon
    in time of deep despair,
He knows our many heartaches,
    He sees our every care.

There is One who sees each tear that falls
    And feels each throbbing pain;
He longs to draw us close to Him
    And revive our soul again.

Dear friend, this One I tell you of,
    Sweet Jesus is His name;
No matter what besets the soul
    He's always just the same.

So lean upon His strength today,
    He'll bring you safely through.
For when the night seems the darkest
    His love will rescue you.

               Barbara Thompson Young

If any little thought of ours
Can make one life the stronger;
If any cheery smile of ours
Can make its brightness longer;
Then let us speak that thought today,
With tender eyes aglowing,
So God may grant some weary one
Shall reap from our glad sowing.

Lord Keep Me Going

Lord keep me going for another day,
And when this body languishes for rest,
Bring peaceful sleep throughout the quiet hours,
Unmarred by worries and by restlessness.
Lord keep me going when my back becomes
Too sore to bear the burden of it all,
When vision dims, and everywhere I turn,
It seems I only bump into a wall.

Lord keep me going when the way becomes
Overgrown with brambles and with weeds,
Turn not Thy face away, I ask for naught
Save Thou attend to my most meager needs.
And if sometimes I may be sad of heart,
I beg at least, dear Lord, keep it from showing.
I do not ask to walk upon the waves,
But for another day, Lord keep me going.

Grace E. Easley

No Prayer Goes Unheard

Often we pause and wonder
    When we kneel down to pray —
Can God really hear
    The prayers that we say . . .
But if we keep praying
    And talking to Him,
He'll brighten the soul
    That was clouded and dim,
And as we continue
    Our burden seems lighter,
Our sorrow is softened
    And our outlook is brighter

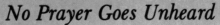

For though we feel helpless
    And alone when we start,
Our prayer is the key
    That opens the heart,
And as our heart opens
    The dear Lord comes in
And the prayer that we felt
    We could never begin
Is so easy to say
    For the Lord understands
And gives us new strength
    By the touch of His hands.

    Helen Steiner Rice

GETHSEMANE

Forlorn I was, as I knelt to pray,
    I could not drive my cares away;
It seemed that life was all in vain,
    Sunshine gone, just freezing rain.

I cried for mercy in my strife,
    That God would bless my daily life,
That somehow I could find the way
    To hold my troubles all at bay.

Then I heard a voice, and tenderly,
    "Is this then, your Gethsemane?"
And then I knew the love He bore
    Would guide my veering ship to shore.

I knew my cares were pretty small,
    In Gethsemane He gave His all,
And who was I to kneel, and feel
    His love could not all sorrow heal?

I thanked Him with a grateful heart,
    And rose to make a better start,
With faith to walk the path He trod,
    In joy to rest in the Lap of God.

I knew that from this day till death
    I'd sing His praise with every breath,
For how could I linger in Gethsemane
    With His gentle hand to quicken me?

                W. R. Goodman

A Plea for Serenity

God, mold my spirit whole again,
And grant me peace of mind.
Please calm my secret doubts and fears,
Then courage I will find
To face the ever-changing tide —
Darkest night or dreary day,
Knowing that You're guiding me,
Always near me lest I stray.

                    Gorda Jeffcoat

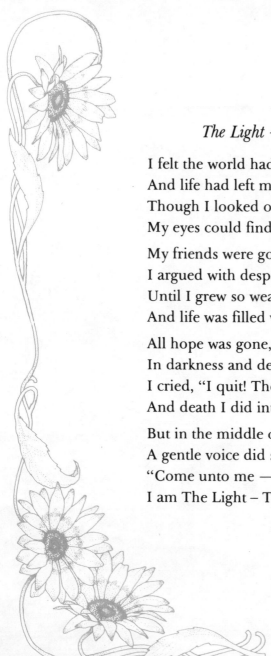

The Light – The Way

I felt the world had turned me down
And life had left me low;
Though I looked on every side,
My eyes could find but woe.

My friends were gone, and all alone
I argued with despair;
Until I grew so weak and worn
And life was filled with care.

All hope was gone, and as I walked
In darkness and defeat,
I cried, "I quit! There's no way out!"
And death I did intreat.

But in the middle of my darkness
A gentle voice did say:
"Come unto me — no need to fear
I am The Light – The Way.

Though trouble walks on every side,
I shall dwell within
To strengthen and protect you
And keep your heart from sin."

The choice was mine, to live or die,
To lose, or ever win;
Without a word, I fell at His feet,
Such peace there came within.

Somehow I knew that I could be
Whatever He should bid,
And on my feet I stood and said,
"I shall not die, but live!"

Now when I'm tested, tossed and tried,
I still can hear Him say,
"Come unto me, no need to fear,
I am The Light – The Way."

Barbara Thompson Young

RESOLVE

To strip the soul of all pretense,
    To hold each day in reverence,
To keep the head and heart apace,
    To make this world a worth-while place,
To share my bread with those in need,
    To tolerate a neighbor's creed,
To keep a stride without a strut,
    To make a home in manse or hut,
To have the grit to grin at loss,
    To master life and be its boss!

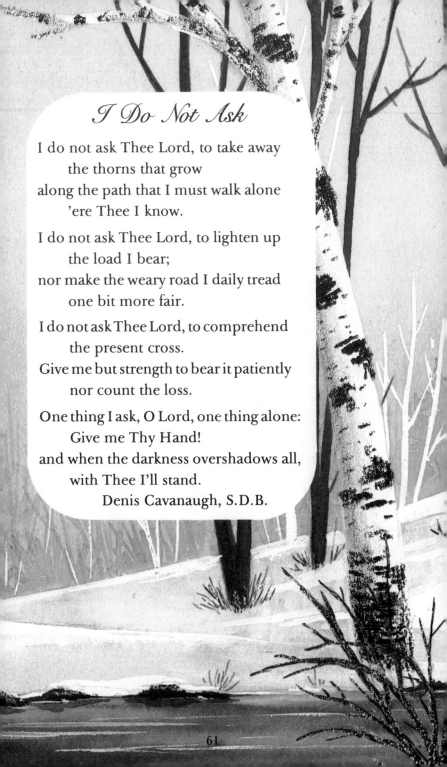

I Do Not Ask

I do not ask Thee Lord, to take away
    the thorns that grow
along the path that I must walk alone
    'ere Thee I know.

I do not ask Thee Lord, to lighten up
    the load I bear;
nor make the weary road I daily tread
    one bit more fair.

I do not ask Thee Lord, to comprehend
    the present cross.
Give me but strength to bear it patiently
    nor count the loss.

One thing I ask, O Lord, one thing alone:
    Give me Thy Hand!
and when the darkness overshadows all,
    with Thee I'll stand.
            Denis Cavanaugh, S.D.B.

Lord Help Me Today

Lord help me today,
To give a cheery smile;
Lord help me today,
To go the second mile;
Lord help me today,
Not to seek worldly fame;
Lord help me today,
To praise Thy holy name.

Lord help me today,
To be a shining light;
Lord help me today,
To know the wrong from right;

Lord help me today,
In each and every way.
Lord help me today,
To seek you when I pray.

Ronald A. Bond

Desert Sand

My life was a desert full of sand,
The sun burned down to scorch the land,
No vegetation grew in me,
Just stones, and sand, and misery.

But then there came a healing rain:
God set my gloomy heart aflame,
And, from the burning sand, there grew
Green grass, and flowers of every hue.

He watered it with magic love,
And tuned my heart to look above,
And, in the sunshine of His smile,
My empty life became worthwhile.

He caused the sand, once in repose,
In love, to blossom like the rose,
The barren earth to sprout, and grow,
Where e'er His Living Waters flow!

                    W. R. Goodman

BY FAITH ALONE

When I recall the blessings
    God has scattered all along my way,
The unexpected little joys
    That form the fiber of each day,
When I remember lovely things
    That turn the greyest skies to blue,
A ray of sunlight seems to fall
    Among the hills I wander through.

When my fumbling fingers find,
    Despite all wisdom and all wit,
That many of the pieces of
    Life's puzzle do not seem to fit,

He has a way of sorting out
　　The interlocking shapes for me,
Until the pattern falls in place,
　　Aligned in perfect symmetry.

And so it is forevermore,
　　And I must trust His guiding hand,
His wonderous ways that reach beyond
　　All I can hope to understand.
The instances of faith restored,
　　Of hope renewed and love received,
Are all that is required for one
　　. . . Who has not seen and yet believed.

　　　　　　　　Grace E. Easley

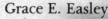

A New Day

Dusk falls . . . and I close my eyes
    To wake to a bright new tomorrow.
Gone are . . . the labors of life, the
    futility of strife, and the
    lingering trauma of sorrow.
Dawn breaks . . . and I clearly see
    A new day of heavenly creation
Fresh with new hope, renewed faith
    and good cheer, and the promise
    of eternal salvation.

                Dolores Karides

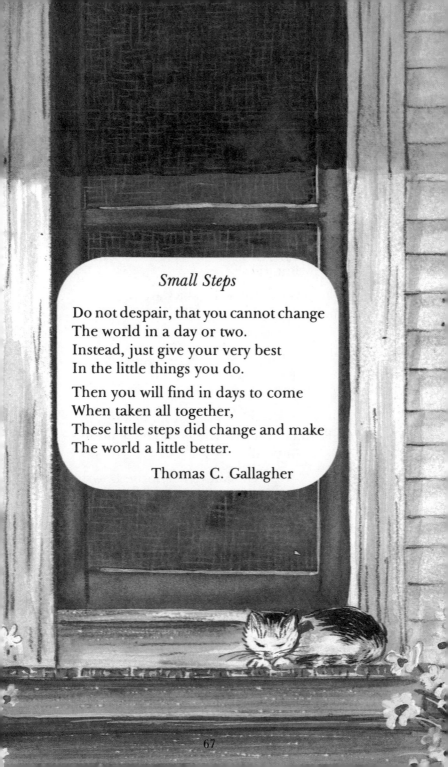

Small Steps

Do not despair, that you cannot change
The world in a day or two.
Instead, just give your very best
In the little things you do.

Then you will find in days to come
When taken all together,
These little steps did change and make
The world a little better.

Thomas C. Gallagher

But Didn't

Do you ever think at close of day
Of kindly words you meant to say —
      But didn't?

Do you ever think when day is done
Of errands kind you could have run —
      But didn't?

Do you ever think at daytime's leave
Of flowers gay you meant to give —
      But didn't?

Do you ever think when skies are red
Of hungry mouths you could have fed —
      But didn't?

Do you ever think at dawn of night
Of letters kind you meant to write —
      But didn't?

Friend, do you think at life's set of sun
You'll think of deeds you could have done —
      But didn't?

Kathryn Thorne Bowsher

At the Feet of Love

Like Martha
reason is troubled
and complains
of many things;
like Mary
faith sits silent
and listens
at the feet of Love.

Edward A.
Gloeggler

69

The Blessings of Trust

Trust gives a purpose
>To our earthly life.
Makes it rewarding,
>And well worth the strife.
The virtue of trust
>Can free us from care,
The lever of trust
>Can lift from despair.
Trust calms troubled minds
>In times of distress,
It serves as a balm
>To soothe and to bless.
It's a safety valve
>For our emotions,
It controls our acts
>In great commotions.
It's a dynamo
>Of Divine Power
That brings strength to us
>In our weakest hour.
It sheds an aura
>Of love and of peace,
It makes discontent
>And resentments cease.

Sister Mary Gemma Brunke

70

GOD HEALS

For each and every aching heart
    In this old world today
There is a cure – one safe and sure:
    Just this – learn how to pray.

Pour out your aching heart to Him
    Who understands and cares;
He is the only one who knows,
    The only one who shares.

God can – and does – heal broken hearts,
    And gives us life anew;
He's ready – waiting – for your prayers;
    He'll do it now – for you.

              Mary Lavinia Silvia

Song of a
Good Samaritan

I cannot sail across the seas
    to work with people there —
but, still, I know it's up to me
    to give and gladly share.

I may not follow jungle paths
    or teach in distant lands —
But, still, there are some people here
    who need my loving hands.

I'll never chant by calm lagoons
    beneath a full-moon sky —
but, still, I shall fulfill my goal
    if I, before I die,

forget to walk horizon's edge
    in seeking destiny
and help the person I can see
    who is in front of me.

        Eugene G. E. Botelho

Two Roads

The road of life is the road we take
In our everyday thoughts and deeds,
A selfish road for the most of us
Made of our own joys and needs.

The road of prayer, on the other hand,
Is the road we take at night
When we blindly grope for the Hand of God
And beg for His guiding light.

A mortal travels the saints' own road
On Heaven's great thoroughfare
When the road of his life is blended with
The wonderful Road of Prayer.

Nick Kenny

BOUNTIFUL BLESSING

May the greatest of gifts come and linger
    With us and our loved ones today,
To bring us the sunshine of gladness
    And banish all sadness away;
To guard all the ways of the future,
    To light all the paths we have trod:
For the greatest of gifts and of treasures
    Is the bountiful blessing of God.

Brian O'Higgins

CONDEMNATION

Until you've walked a second mile
    In someone else's shoes,
Or stood an hour in the heat
    Of hurts you did not choose;
Until your heart has felt the sting
    Of criticizing tongue,
You cannot taste the salty tears
    A wounded soul has wrung.

Unless you've walked a moon or more
    Along a thorny road,
You cannot feel another's need
    To know his trying load.

                Roxie Lusk Smith

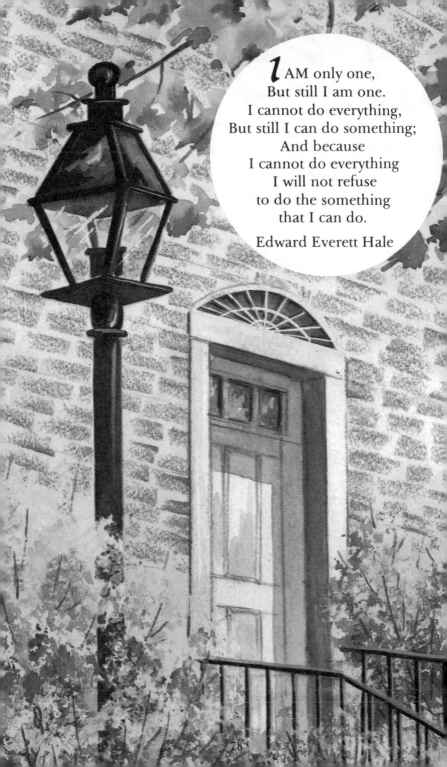

I AM only one,
But still I am one.
I cannot do everything,
But still I can do something;
And because
I cannot do everything
I will not refuse
to do the something
that I can do.

Edward Everett Hale

Things that Never Die

The pure, the bright, the beautiful
    That stirred our hearts in youth,
The impulses to wordless prayer,
    The streams of love and truth,
The longing after something lost,
    The spirit's yearning cry,
The striving after better hopes —
    These things can never die.

The timid hand stretched forth to aid
    A brother in his need;
A kindly word in grief's dark hour
    That proves a friend indeed;
The plea for mercy softly breathed,
    When justice threatens high,
The sorrow of a contrite heart —
    These things shall never die.

Let nothing pass, for every hand
    Must find some work to do,
Lose not a chance to waken love —
    Be firm and just and true.
So shall a light that cannot fade
    Beam on thee from on high,
And angel voices say to thee —
    "These things shall never die."

Charles Dickens

The Prayer Perfect

Dear Lord! Kind Lord!
    Gracious Lord! I pray
Thou wilt look on all I love,
    Tenderly today!

Weed their hearts of weariness;
    Scatter every care
Down a wake of angel-wings
    Winnowing the air.

Bring unto the sorrowing
    All release from pain;
Let the lips of laughter
    Overflow again;

And with all the needy
    O divide, I pray,
This vast treasure of content
    That is mine today!

        James Whitcomb Riley

THE LESSON OF THE YEARS

The years have taught me many things
    But none so sure as this:
That shelter, solace, joy and strength
    Are always where God is.

So now when hope and courage fail,
    And only fear is strong,
My heart will sing as in the past
    An unforgotten song.

God is my refuge and my strength
    I will not be afraid,
And though the night be wild and dark
    I'll meet it undismayed.

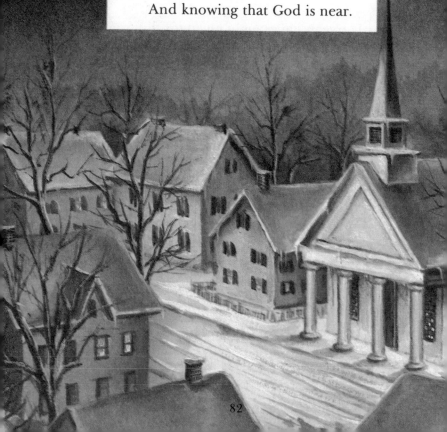

FAITH

Faith is the eye that sees God,
    No matter how dark the day.
Faith is the hand that holds Him
    On the steep and rugged way.

Faith is the heart rejoicing —
    Accepting God's promise true.
Faith is the ear that listens,
    To the voice that speaks to you.

Faith refuses to doubt Him,
    Though others are filled with fear,
Faith is believing the Word,
    And knowing that God is near.

Forgive Me, Lord

Forgive me Lord, for all my wrongs,
    I need Your help, to keep me strong.
I need Your love from day to day,
    To show me how, to find my way.

The night is dark, and I am sad,
    I pray to Thee, to make me glad.
In heaven above, I hope to be
    To worship You, for eternity.

For all my sins, I feel contrite,
    A deep desire, to set things right.
In humble prayer, I ask Your grace,
    My only dream, in heaven, a place.

And thru my life stay by my side,
    In all my needs, be Thou my guide
To help me find, in faith above,
    That peace of mind, which comes with love.

                Francis X. Wadland

Show Me the Way

Show me how to carry, Lord,
This cross you've given me,
Help me never to forget
That day on Calvary.

You carried such a heavy cross,
And though three times You fell —
You got up and walked again
And carried Your cross well.

But being just a simple soul,
Without the strength you've known,
I'm not sure I can carry
This heavy cross alone.

So Lord, if You should see me
Stumble now and then —
Give me the strength and courage
To get up and walk again.

Doris A. Orth

God's Extras

God could have made the sun to rise
    Without such splendor in the skies;
He could have made the sun to set
    Without a glory greater yet.

He could have made the corn to grow
    Without the sunny, golden glow;
The fruit without those colors bright,
    So pleasant to the taste and sight.

He could have made the ocean roll
    Without such music for the soul —
The mighty anthem, loud and strong —
    And birds without their clear, sweet song.

The God who fashioned flow'rs and trees,
    Delights to give us things that please,
And all His handiwork so fair
    His glory and His love declare.

Yes, He Who made the earth and skies
    Gave "extras" for our ears and eyes,
And while my heart with rapture sings,
    I thank Him for the "extra things."

Margaret K. Frazer

TRUST

The way of life seems dark,
And, yet, within my heart I know,
Though I stumble and might fall,
The light of Truth
Will guide me on my way,
If I but heed its call.

Laura Stahl

TAKE TIME

Take time for prayer in the morning
   Take time for prayer at night
Take time for God and through the day
   He'll see that things go right.

      And if you should encounter
         A few mishaps along your way
      He'll surely give you strength and help
         To get you through your day.

And then when evening befalls you
   And you come to the end of the day
He'll still be there to hear your prayer
   And listen to all you say.

      You'll feel His hand of comfort
         As you talk with Him once more
      And thank Him for His loving care
         And blessing by the score.

So take time for God in the morning
   Take time for God at night
And talk with God, and walk with God
   He'll make your burden light.

                  Florence Flett

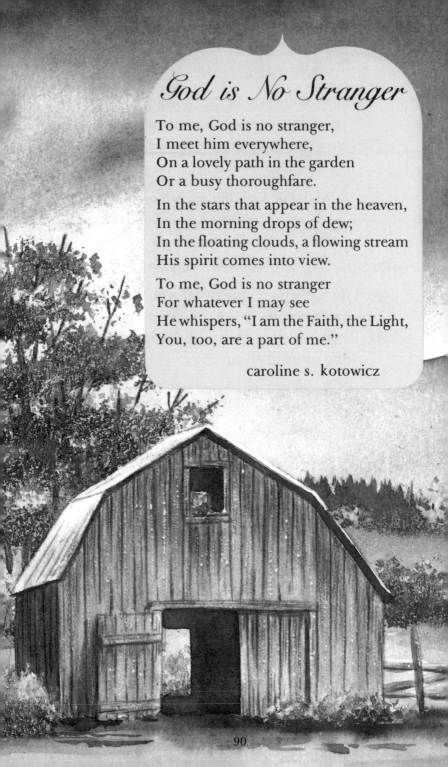

God is No Stranger

To me, God is no stranger,
I meet him everywhere,
On a lovely path in the garden
Or a busy thoroughfare.

In the stars that appear in the heaven,
In the morning drops of dew;
In the floating clouds, a flowing stream
His spirit comes into view.

To me, God is no stranger
For whatever I may see
He whispers, "I am the Faith, the Light,
You, too, are a part of me."

caroline s. kotowicz

All Things by Him

We're surrounded by so many things
    Of wonder and of worth
Created by our King of Kings
    A Heaven right here on earth.

And, as we look about
    And view all things that be
His work in every earthly thing
    Proof of Eternity.

Take winter with its magic spell
    A landscape clothed in white
Or the summer breeze we love so well
    Whispering softly thru the night.

All things are here by His creation
    Land, the water and our birth
Our every sense His illustration
    Of perfection here on earth.

The awesome marvel of it all
    By our architect Supreme
This haven created for one and all
    Where life would be the theme.

We honor Him and offer thanks
    For each blessing He bestowed
The teachings of His Savior Son
    For all the only road.

                Joseph G. Pearce

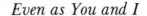

Even as You and I

A frightened flower caught within
    A raging storm bent down its head,
It drooped in languishment, and I
    Thought surely morn would find it dead
But with the sun it raised its face,
    Its petaled heart half torn with pain,
And do you know its fragrance was
    So much the sweeter for the rain!

              Esther Nilsson

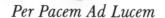

Per Pacem Ad Lucem

I do not ask, O Lord, that life may be
A pleasant road;
I do not ask that Thou wouldst take from me
Aught of its load;

I do not ask that flowers should always spring
Beneath my feet;
I know too well the poison and the sting
Of things too sweet.

For one thing only, Lord, dear Lord, I plead,
Lead me aright—
Though strength should falter, and though
        heart should bleed—
Through Peace to Light.

I do not ask, O Lord, that Thou shouldst shed
Full radiance here;
Give but a ray of peace, that I may tread
Without a fear.

I do not ask my cross to understand,
My way to see;
Better in darkness just to feel Thy Hand
And follow Thee.

Joy is like restless day; but peace divine
Like quiet night:
Lead me, O Lord, — till perfect Day shall
        shine,
Through Peace to Light.

                Adelaide Anne Procter

God's Will

I know
not by what
methods rare,
But this I know:
God answers prayer.
I know
not if the blessing
sought will come in just
the guise I thought.
I leave my prayer
to Him alone
Whose will is wiser
than my own.

Eliza M. Hickok

BECAUSE

Because I have received kindness,
    I have been spurred on to be kind.

Because I have caught the smile
      on another's lips,
    I have found myself smiling.

Because I have known
      the joy of receiving,
    I rejoice in giving.

Because I have felt pain,
    I know what pity is.

Because I have tasted humiliations,
    I know what consideration is.

Because I have seen Christ suffer,
    I have had the courage to go on.

                Sister Mary Gemma Brunke

God's Work of Art

There's so much beauty to be found
    In this world of ours —
In winding streams and fields of green,
    And oh, so many flowers.

In fluffy clouds – like "cotton puffs",
    And skies of azure hue.
There's beauty in the rolling hills,
    And God's green valleys too.

There's beauty in a tree's attempt
    To reach majestic height.
There's beauty in the sunshine
    And the moon and stars at night.

Surely beauty such as this
    Could only have been planned,
And brought into existence
    By God's own loving hand!

Doris A. Orth

My Prayer at Dawn

I pray this day will brightly shine
    With little deeds well done,
And thoughtful love for others,
    So that the setting sun
And all the lengthening shadows
    Will bring a peaceful rest,
Knowing that God guided me
    To truly do my best.

Mary H. Wittner

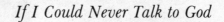

If I Could Never Talk to God

I often wonder what I'd do
    If I could never pray,
If I could not depend on God
    To guide me every day.

And o how dark the night would be
    If His light did not shine,
I could not sleep because such fear
    Would fill this heart of mine.

My heart would never sing a song
    I'd feel so all alone,
If I could never talk to God
    And claim Him for my own.

But all these things I need not fear
    My burdens He doth share,
I only have to whisper low
    He heareth every prayer.

Thus He always walks beside me
    · He never lets me fall,
He gently takes me by the hand
    My love, the God of all.

And though the night around be dark
    His light will ever shine,
I sleep in peace and need not fear
    Since I know that He is mine.

             Mary E. Harrington

Life's Fulfillment

Of all the prizes that earth can give
This is the best; to find Thee, Lord,
A living Presence near and in Thee rest!

Friends, fortune, fame
Or what might come to me —
I count all loss if I find not
Companionship with Thee!

Ralph Spaulding Cushman

Let Not Your Heart Be Troubled

Whenever I am troubled
    and lost in deep despair
I bundle all my troubles up
    and go to God in prayer . . .

I tell him I am heartsick
    and lost and lonely, too,
That my mind is deeply burdened
    and I don't know what to do . . .

But I know He stilled the tempest
    and calmed the angry sea
And I humbly ask if in His Love
    He'll do the same for me . . .

And then I just keep quiet
    and think only thoughts of peace
And if I abide in stillness
    my "restless murmurings" cease.

Helen Steiner Rice

This Worry

If you could take this worry
    That is eating at your heart,
Wrap it up, and throw it away,
    Then from it completely depart,–

Wouldn't this just be wonderful,–
    Imagine the great relief,
The quietness within your heart,
    The restfulness and peace!

My friend, this all is possible
    Thru our Savior Jesus Christ,
The One Who would take each burden
    That comes into our life.

So wrap your every burden up
    And give it over to Him
Who promises, when we trust Him,
    To give God's Peace within!

Ruth V. Eaker

1 Corinthians 10:13; Philippians 4:6 & 7

104

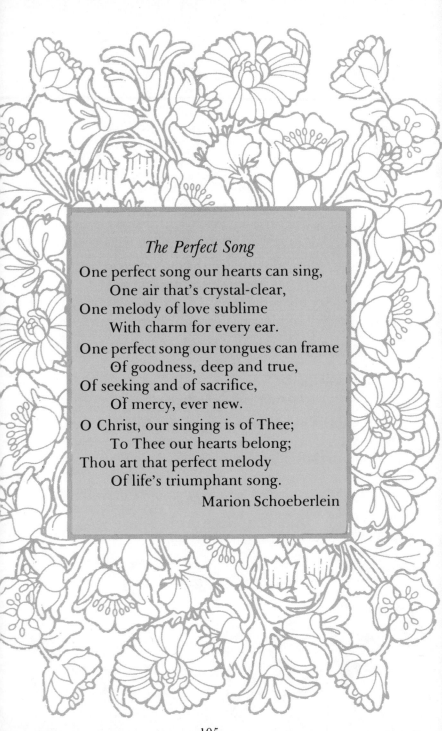

The Perfect Song

One perfect song our hearts can sing,
    One air that's crystal-clear,
One melody of love sublime
    With charm for every ear.

One perfect song our tongues can frame
    Of goodness, deep and true,
Of seeking and of sacrifice,
    Of mercy, ever new.

O Christ, our singing is of Thee;
    To Thee our hearts belong;
Thou art that perfect melody
    Of life's triumphant song.

                Marion Schoeberlein

Light Shining Out of Darkness

God moved in a mysterious way
    His wonders to perform;
He plants His footsteps in the sea,
    And rides upon the storm.

Deep in unfathomable mines
    Of never-failing skill
He treasures up His bright designs,
    And works His sovereign will.

Ye fearful saints, fresh courage take;
    The clouds ye so much dread
Are big with mercy, and shall break
    In blessings on your head.

Judge not the Lord by feeble sense,
    But trust Him for His grace;
Behind a frowning providence
    He hides a smiling face.

His purposes will ripen fast,
    Unfolding every hour;
The bud may have a bitter taste,
    But sweet will be the flower.

Blind unbelief is sure to err,
    And scan His work in vain;
God is His own interpreter,
    And He will make it plain.

                William Cowper

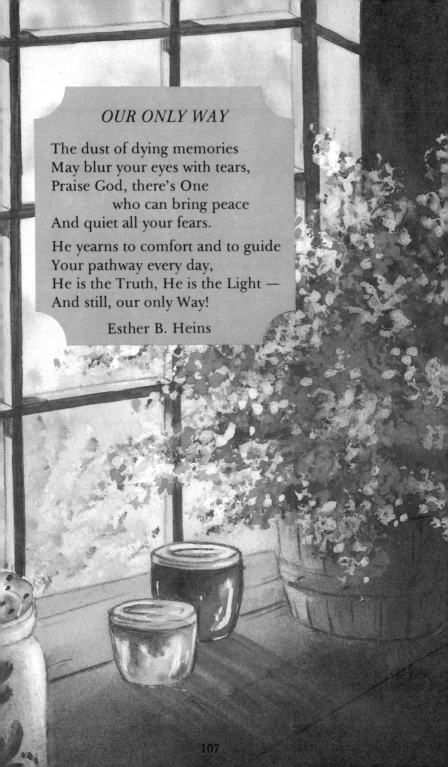

OUR ONLY WAY

The dust of dying memories
May blur your eyes with tears,
Praise God, there's One
       who can bring peace
And quiet all your fears.

He yearns to comfort and to guide
Your pathway every day,
He is the Truth, He is the Light —
And still, our only Way!

      Esther B. Heins

Living Water

That none need
suffer in spirit
His agony of thirst
on the cross,
to all that ask
He gives
living water
of the Spirit.

Edward A. Gloeggler

May your faith in God
        sustain you
In time of grief and pain,
For faith in God that you possess
    Is never placed in vain.

God's always standing by your side
    In moments of despair,
To strengthen and to comfort you
    For He does truly care.

He's always there to lend a hand
    And be your friend and guide,
So don't believe you walk alone
    For God walks by your side.

Harold F. Mohn

BY THE SEA

I walked alone beside the sea;
    And as I walked there seemed to be;
An unseen Friend walked by my side
    As I wondered at the changing tide.

He rules the sea, the sky, the land,
    The moon and stars hear His command.
All else, but man, joins His melody
    Of love and faith and harmony.

His gentle voice spoke from the sea,
"Be not afraid, just follow me."
I noticed not the time or way
As we walked and talked that day.

I lingered there until the sun
Dipped in the sea, and day was done.
My cares, my fears all slipped away,
Because I walked with Him that day.

I hurried home, by duty called,
All seemed right within its walls.
My hope renewed, tears washed away
Because I talked with God that day.

Grace Holt Litchfield

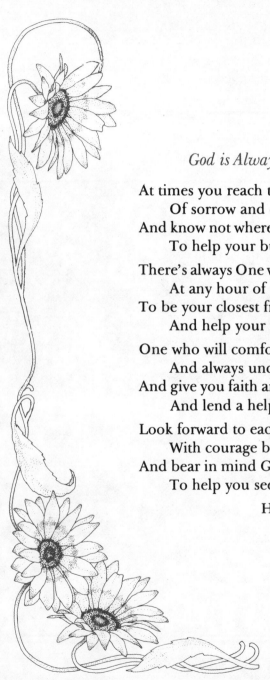

God is Always There

At times you reach the bottom
　　Of sorrow and despair,
And know not where to turn for aid
　　To help your burdens bear.

There's always One who's standing by
　　At any hour of day,
To be your closest friend and guide
　　And help your fears allay.

One who will comfort and sustain
　　And always understand,
And give you faith and inner strength
　　And lend a helping hand.

Look forward to each new born day
　　With courage born anew.
And bear in mind God's always there
　　To help you see it through.

　　　　　　　　Harold F. Mohn

The Heavens Declare
Thy Glory, Lord!

The heavens declare Thy glory, Lord!
In every star Thy wisdom shines;
That when our eyes behold Thy word,
We read Thy name in fairer lines.

The rolling sun, the changing light
And nights and days Thy power confess;
That the blest volume Thou has writ
Reveals Thy justice and Thy grace.

(Psalm XIX)

Isaac Watts

The Power of Littles

Great events, we often find,
    On little things depend,
And very small beginnings
    Have oft a mighty end.

A single utterance may good
    Or evil thought inspire;
One little spark enkindled
    May set a town on fire.

What volumes may be written
    With little drops of ink!
How small a leak, unnoticed,
    A mighty ship will sink!

Our life is made entirely
    Of moments multiplied,
As little streamlets, joining,
    Form the ocean's tide.

Our hours and days,
      our months and years,
    Are in small moments given:
They constitute our time below —
    Eternity in heaven.

In Sunshine or Rain

He walks with me in sunshine bright,
    When skies are blue and all is right.
And when I tread dark valley deep,
    My Loving Lord my steps doth keep.

In darkest night my Lord is near;
    He whispers, "peace," dispelling fear.
And when my heart knows dark despair,
    He calms my soul, my sorrows share.

In joy or grief my Lord abides,
    And ever in my heart resides –
How blest am I that Christ doth deign
    To walk with me, sunshine or rain!

Kathryn Thorne Bowsher

I Thought of a Rainbow

I thought of a rainbow today,
    As I watched the rain coming down,
Someday my life would be better,
    I would not be all alone.

The sparrows in November trees
    Seemed so discouraged, just like me—
I think that they were looking for
    God's little bit of poetry—

No matter where I looked beauty
    And nature preached a sermon, though,
Even in dark discouragement
    I saw HIS beautiful rainbow!

             Marion Schoeberlein

Life's Tapestry

Glancing at the pattern
    Of my life's rare tapestry
It seemed the threads of darkness
    Were all that I could see,

I failed to see the glitter
    Of the gold beyond the grey
The myriad lovely colours
    Of life's joys along the way,

Until I saw the pattern
    Formed by God's forgiving touch
That showed me, Oh so clearly
    God has given me so much.

             Gert Holaday

Cultivating Friends

Sow a word of praise today,
    Plant a kindness-seed;
Listen to a troubled friend,
    Help someone in need.

Compliment a weary soul
    Too fatigued to try;
Shine forth rays of hope on all,
    Comfort those who cry.

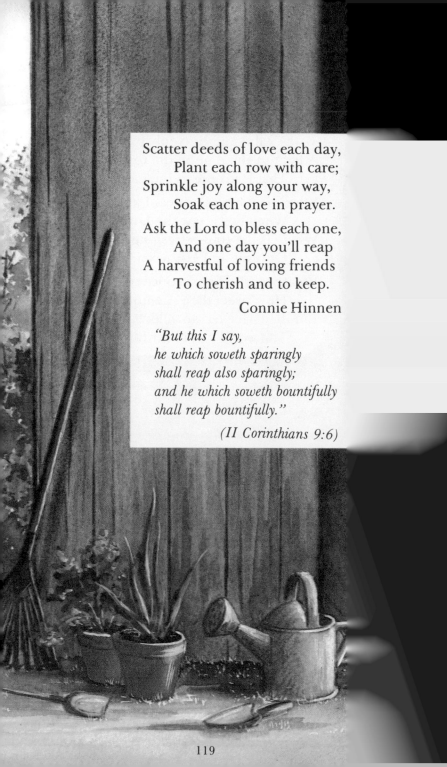

Scatter deeds of love each day,
    Plant each row with care;
Sprinkle joy along your way,
    Soak each one in prayer.

Ask the Lord to bless each one,
    And one day you'll reap
A harvestful of loving friends
    To cherish and to keep.

              Connie Hinnen

"But this I say,
he which soweth sparingly
shall reap also sparingly;
and he which soweth bountifully
shall reap bountifully."

           (II Corinthians 9:6)

WALKING WITH GOD

O for a closer walk with God,
A calm and heavenly frame,
A light to shine upon the road
That leads me to the Lamb!

Where is the blessedness I knew
When first I saw the Lord?
Where is the soul-refreshing view
Of Jesus and His word?

What peaceful hours I once enjoy'd!
How sweet their memory still!
But they have left an aching void,
The world can never fill.

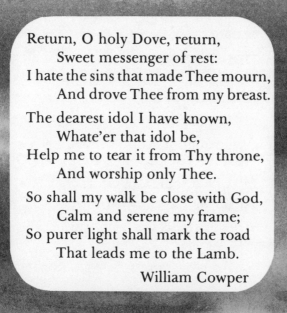

Return, O holy Dove, return,
   Sweet messenger of rest:
I hate the sins that made Thee mourn,
   And drove Thee from my breast.

The dearest idol I have known,
   Whate'er that idol be,
Help me to tear it from Thy throne,
   And worship only Thee.

So shall my walk be close with God,
   Calm and serene my frame;
So purer light shall mark the road
   That leads me to the Lamb.

           William Cowper

In Quietude

I know not how by hand or arm
God sweetly doth console;
It's not by worldly happenstance
He pacifies my soul . . .
Deep within, there cometh peace —
A child of His I be —
He worketh all to my own good
And sets my spirit free —
What ere I am, God views the whole;
My wilted soul takes wing!
He lifts to bless my earthly ways
What heaven's best can bring.

Roxie Lusk Smith

NOBILITY

True worth is in being, not seeming, —
 In doing, each day that goes by,
Some little good — not in dreaming
 Of great things to do by and by.

For whatever men say in their blindness,
 And spite of the fancies of youth,
There's nothing so kingly as kindness,
 And nothing so royal as truth.

We get back our mete as we measure —
 We cannot do wrong and feel right,
Nor can we give pain and gain pleasure,
 For justice avenges each slight.

We cannot make bargains for blisses,
 Nor catch them like fishes in nets;
And sometimes the thing our life misses
 Helps more than the thing which it gets.

For good lieth not in pursuing,
 Nor gaining of great nor of small,
But just in the doing, and doing
 As we would be done by, is all.

Alice Cary

He Loves You!

It's amazing and incredible,
　　But it's as true as it can be,
God loves and understands us all
　　And that means you and me —

His grace is all sufficient
　　For both the young and old,
For the lonely and the timid,
　　For the brash and for the bold —

His love knows no exceptions,
　　So never feel excluded,
No matter who or what you are
　　Your name has been included —

And no matter what your past has been
　　Trust God to understand
And no matter what your problem is
　　Just place it in his Hand —

For in all of our unloveliness
　　This great God loves us still,
He loved us since the world began
　　And what's more, He always will!

　　　　　　　　Helen Steiner Rice

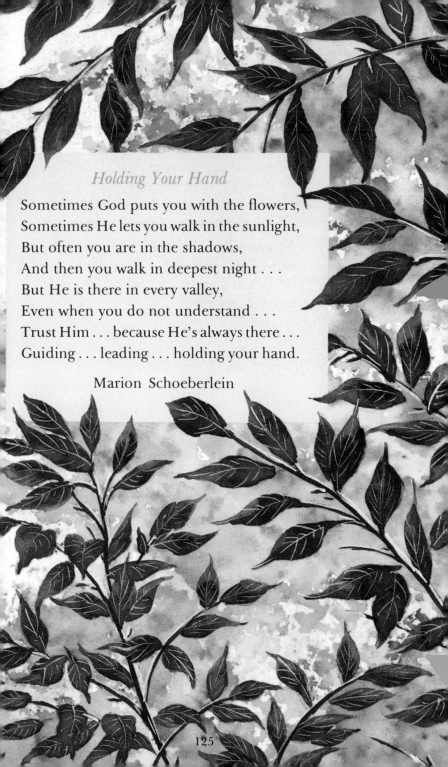

Holding Your Hand

Sometimes God puts you with the flowers,
Sometimes He lets you walk in the sunlight,
But often you are in the shadows,
And then you walk in deepest night . . .
But He is there in every valley,
Even when you do not understand . . .
Trust Him . . . because He's always there . . .
Guiding . . . leading . . . holding your hand.

Marion Schoeberlein

The Half I Cannot Tell

My heart is overflowing
    With gratitude and praise,
To him whose loving kindness
    Has followed all my days;
To him who gently leads me
    By cool and quiet rills,
And with their balm of comfort
    My thirsty spirit fills.

I feign would tell the story,
And yet I know full well
The half was never, never told –
The half I cannot tell.

Within the vale of blessing,
  I walk beneath the light
Reflected from His glory,
  That shines forever bright.
I feel His constant presence
  Wherever I may be;
How manifold His goodness,
  How rich His grace to me!

My heart is overflowing
  With love and joy and song,
As if it heard an echo
  From yonder ransomed throng;
Its every chord is vocal
  With music's sweetest lay;
And to its home of sunshine
  It longs to fly away.

                    Fanny Crosby

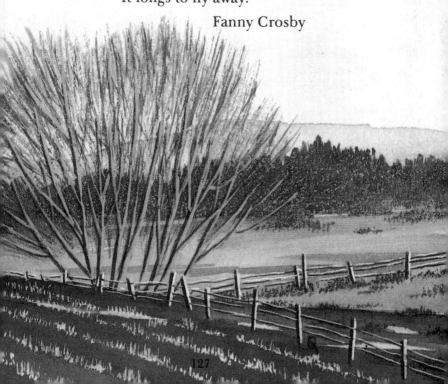

127

After the Darkness

After the darkness
The daylight shines through
After the showers
The rainbow's in view
After life's heartaches
There comes from above
The peace and the comfort
of God's healing love.